AF444527

Spruce Bough
Poems

Also by H. G. Moser

Still Waters, Haiku for the Journey

Birds And Dogs, Selected Poems

Above the Rise, On Fish And Fishing

Edges Rounded, Selected Poems and Prose

Lattice Windows, Structural Poems

Just Lattices, Selected Structural Poems

Aran's Cave, A novella

Lattice World, Selected Structural Poems

Matrix Poetry

Cherry River Poems

Poems For Molly

Other Poems

Last Winter's Poems

Bend Pool Poems

Hazel Tree Poems

Cottonwood Poems

Prairie River Poems

Dream Meadow Poems

Trout's Dream Poems

In Stream Poems

Molly's Hill Poems

Spruce Bough
Poems

H. G. MOSER

Front Cover: Photo of spruce bough by author

In memory of Henrietta and Auntie Mabel,
for the loving care they gave us, and for spruce forests
and the brooks that flow within them

CONTENTS

Perspective

Sometimes you need

to actually be within

a problem to fix it

Cleaner

After a long awaited house cleaning and throwing away lots
of things it takes more time to realize you did not need them
than it takes to forget why you had them in the first place

Day

A day went by what did I

do what could I have done

what could I have noticed

Edge Affect

E   D   G   E   E   D   G   E   E   D   G   E   E
E   D
G   G
D   E
E   E
G   D
D   G
E   E
E   E
G   D
D   G
E   E
E   E   G   D   E   E   G   D   E   E   G   D   E

Simplify

The less you do the
easier it is to know
what you are doing

At Center

C   E   N   T   E   R   C

R   C   E   N   T   E   E

E   T   E   R   C   R   N

T   N   R   @   E   C   T

N   E   E   T   N   E   E

E   C   R   E   T   N   R

C   R   E   T   N   E   C

Love

<pre>
E   E   E
  V   V   V
      O   O   O
E   V   O   L   O   V   E
      O   O   O
  V   V   V
E   E   E
</pre>

SPOTONSPOTONSPOTONSPOT
ONSPOTONSPOTONSPOTONSP
OTONSPOTONSPOTONSPOTON
SPOTONSPOTONSPOTONSPOT
ONSPOTONSPOTONSPOTONSP
OTONSPOTONSPOTONSPOTON
SPOTONSPOTONSPOTONSPOT
ONSPOTONSPOTONSPOTONSP
OTONSPOTONSPOTONSPOTON
SPOTONSPOTONSPOTONSPOT
ONSPOTONSPOTONSPOTONSP
OTONSPOTONSPOTONSPOTON
SPOTONSPOTONSPOTONSPOT
ONSPOTONSPOTONSPOTONSP
OTONSPOTONSPOTONSPOTON
SPOTONSPOTONSPOTONSPOT
ONSPOTONSPOTONSPOTONSP
OTONSPOTONSPOTONSPOTON
SPOTONSPOTONSPOTONSPOT
ONSPOTONSPOTONSPOTONSP
OTONSPOTONSPOTONSPOTON
SPOTONSPOTONSPOTONSPOT
ONSPOTONSPOTONSPOTONSP
OTONSPOTONSPOTONSPOTON
SPOTONSPOTONSPOTONSPOT
ONSPOTONSPOTONSPOTONSP
OTONSPOTONSPOTONSPOTON
SPOTONSPOTONSPOTONSPOT
ONSPOTONSPOTONSPOTONSP

New Person

You become a new person every day
it may not seem so but the days add up
and after a while it becomes obvious

<pre>
I   N   P   U   T

I   N   P   U   T

I   N   P   U   T

I   N   P   U   T

I   N   P   U   T

            P

            P

            P

            P

            P

            P

            P
</pre>

HUMANBEINGHUMANBEINGH
UMANBEINGHUMANBEINGHU
MANBEINGHUMANBEINGHUM
ANBEINGHUMANBEINGHUMA
NBEINGHUMANBEINGHUMAN
BEINGHUMANBEINGHUMANB
EINGHUMANBEINGHUMANBE
INGHUMANBEINGHUMANBEI
NGHUMANBEINGHUMANBEIN
GHUMANBEINGHUMANBEING
HUMANBEINGHUMANBEINGH
UMANBEINGHUMANBEINGHU
MANBEINGHUMANBEINGHUM
ANBEINGHUMANBEINGHUMA
NBEINGHUMANBEINGHUMAN
BEINGHUMANBEINGHUMANB
EINGHUMANBEINGHUMANBE
INGHUMANBEINGHUMANBEI
NGHUMANBEINGHUMANBEIN
GHUMANBEINGHUMANBEING
HUMANBEINGHUMANBEINGH
UMANBEINGHUMANBEINGHU
MANBEINGHUMANBEINGHUM
ANBEINGHUMANBEINGHUMA
NBEINGHUMANBEINGHUMAN

Happenstance

<pre>
        H
        A
    P   P
        E
        N
    S   N
    T   C
A   E
</pre>

12

Point

The specimens in the petri dishes

reached a point where life became

indistinguishable from death

DEEP
DEEP
DEEP
DEEP
DEEP
DEEP
DEEP
DEEP
DEEP
DEEP
DEEP
DEEP
DEEP
DEEP
DEEP
DEEP
DEEP
DEEP
DEEP
DEEP
DEEP
DEEP

Copies

Portmanteau

My teacher told me a portmanteau is not a word that refers to
towing a skier from the port side of a boat but a kind of luggage,
usually of stiff leather, that one carries from place to place.

Albert

You have to be
/   —   —   /
unusually smart
/

———

to be a head of
your time

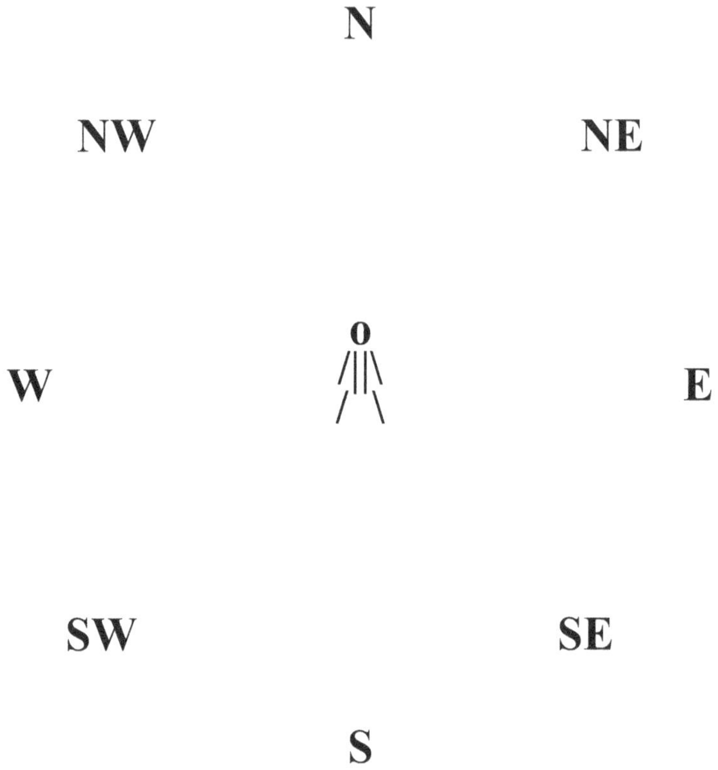

N

NW   NE

o

W   E

SW   SE

S

Almost

A poet friend claimed there
is a poem in everything and
almost everything is a poem

H E A R T   B R E A K

H E A R T   B R E A K

H E A R T   B R E A K

H E A R T   B R E A K

H E A R T   B R E A K

H E A R T   B R E A K

H E A R T   B R E A K

H E A R T   B R E A K

H E A R T   B R E A K

H E A R T   B R E A K

H E A R T   B R E A K

H E A R T   B R E A K

Chocolate

Sometimes you just have to accept
the fact that there is no chocolate
when you're searching for chocolate

Career

It's never too late for

a career change

in fact it's never too late

for a career of any kind

LUGGAGELUGGAGEL
UGGAGELUGGAGELU
GGAGELUGGAGELUG
GAGELUGGAGELUGG
AGELUGGAGELUGGA
GELUGGAGELUGGAG
ELUGGAGELUGGAGE
LUGGAGELUGGAGEL
UGGAGELUGGAGELU
GGAGELUGGAGELUG
GAGELUGGAGELUGG
AGELUGGAGELUGGA
GELUGGAGELUGGAG
ELUGGAGELUGGAGE
LUGGAGELUGGAGEL
UGGAGELUGGAGELU
GGAGELUGGAGELUG
GAGELUGGAGELUGG
AGELUGGAGELUGGA
GELUGGAGELUGGAG
ELUGGAGELUGGAGE

Are

You are where
you live and you
live where you are
non-irrevocably

Bark

The dog awakened barking
from her dream waking me
before my dream had ended

Buzz

They flunked geometry in high school but
their lives turned out to be Busby Berkeley
dance routines each movement accountable

Question

From one vulnerable person

to another:

So, why are you so vulnerable?

Mileage

I've been noticing the odometer in my dashboard is approaching one hundred thousand miles. I seem to be driving a little slower and more carefully. As with other cars, life felt a little different when that milestone arrived—more with me than with the cars.

Snowy Night

The path to happiness had
many forks beginning with
listening to Robert Frost

Pants

Some look good in corduroys
some look good in khakis but
everybody looks good in denim

Level

There are some levels of
nonchalance that maybe
we should not achieve

Info Tech

ITCHINGITCHINGITCHINGI
TCHINGITCHINGITCHINGIT
CHINGITCHINGITCHINGITC
HINGITCHINGITCHINGITCH
INGITCHINGITCHINGITCHI
NGITCHINGITCHINGITCHIN
GITCHINGITCHINGITCHING
ITCHINGITCHINGITCHINGI
TCHINGITCHINGITCHINGIT
CHINGITCHINGITCHINGITC
HINGITCHINGITCHINGITCH
INGITCHINGITCHINGITCHI
NGITCHINGITCHINGITCHIN
GITCHINGITCHINGITCHING
ITCHINGITCHINGITCHINGI
TCHINGITCHINGITCHINGIT
CHINGITCHINGITCHINGITC
HINGITCHINGITCHINGITCH
INGITCHINGITCHINGITCHI
NGITCHINGITCHINGITCHIN
GITCHINGITCHINGITCHING
ITCHINGITCHINGITCHINGI
TCHINGITCHINGITCHINGIT
CHINGITCHINGITCHINGITC
HINGITCHINGITCHINGITCH
INGITCHINGITCHINGITCHI
NGITCHINGITCHINGITCHIN
GITCHINGITCHINGITCHING
ITCHINGITCHINGITCHINGI
TCHINGITCHINGITCHINGIT
CHINGITCHINGITCHINGITC
HINGITCHINGITCHINGITCH
INGITCHINGITCHINGITCHI
NGITCHINGITCHINGITCHIN
GITCHINGITCHINGITCHING

Typos

Life's typos never
get fixed until the
deadline has passed

Saying

The saying says you better fish
or cut bait but neglects to say
anything about who is the bait

Little World

It figures they had it right
riding in the little car with
the song about a little world

Cabin Fever

It keeps getting colder

in here so it must be

getting colder out there

Subtlety

Is subtlety more endearing than
directness or is subtlety the most
direct of all the endearing traits

Solitaire

A cut wheat field I drive by every day has a single crow sitting out in the middle of the field. Crows are social birds, usually in flocks of various sizes. But here's one all by himself in a huge field. He may be feeding on scattered grain from the harvest. If so, where are the other crows? Is he ostracized by the local flocks and forced to lead a singular life? Or maybe he chooses to be alone. I know some humans like that, preferring a solitary life and few interactions with others of their species, content within themselves. Or maybe he's neither, just a good old social crow having some time to himself and it's only a coincidence that I see him out there almost every day. Then again, maybe there is no crow in the middle of the field and I'm just imagining it. I guess I'll never know unless I pull over to the side of the road and walk out there.

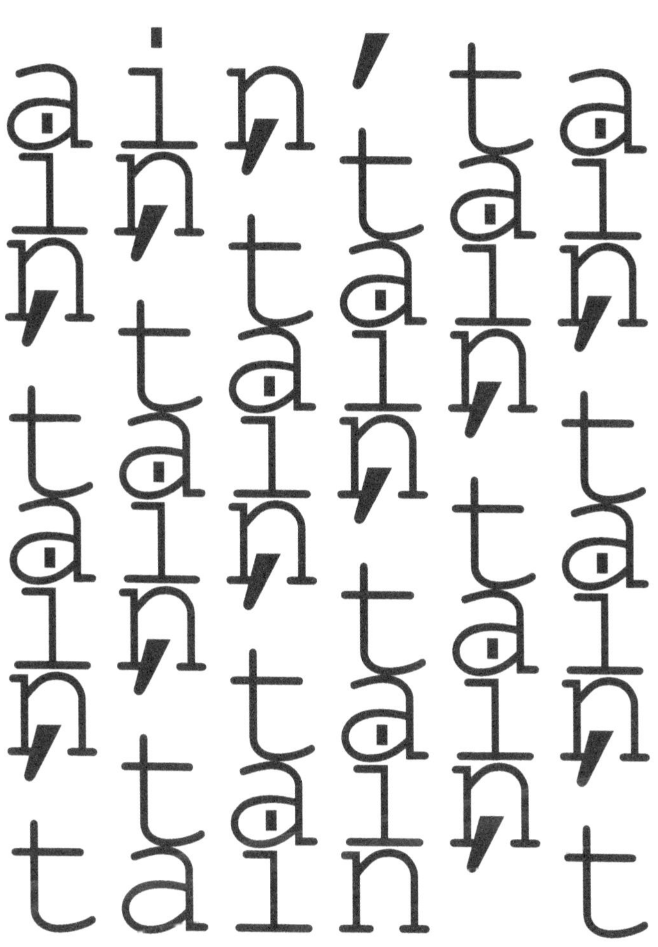

Purrrrrrrrrrrrrrrrrrrrrrrrrrrrrrrrrrrr
rrrrrrrrrrrrrrrrrrrrrrrrrrrrrrrrrrrrr
rrrrrrrrrrrrrrrrrrrrrrrrrrrrrrrrrrrrr
rrrrrrrrrrrrrrrrrrrrrrrrrrrrrrrrrrrrr
rrrrrrrrrrrrrrrrrrrrrrrrrrrrrrrrrrrrr
rrrrrrrrrrrrrrrrrrrrrrrrrrrrrrrrrrrrr
rrrrrrrrrrrrrrrrrrrrrrrrrrrrrrrrrrrrr
rrrrrrrrrrrrrrrrrrrrrrrrrrrrrrrrrrrrr
rrrrrrrrrrrrrrrrrrrrrrrrrrrrrrrrrrrrr
rrrrrrrrrrrrrrrrrrrrrrrrrrrrrrrrrrrrr
rrrrrrrrrrrrrrrrrrrrrrrrrrrrrrrrrrrrr
rrrrrrrrrrrrrrrrrrrrrrrrrrrrrrrrrrrrr
rrrrrrrrrrrrrrrrrrrrrrrrrrrrrrrrrrrrr
rrrrrrrrrrrrrrrrrrrrrrrrrrrrrrrrrrrrr
rrrrrrrrrrrrrrrrrrrrrrrrrrrrrrrrrrrrr
rrrrrrrrrrrrrrrrrrrrrrrrrrrrrrrrrrrrr
rrrrrrrrrrrrrrrrrrrrrrrrrrrrrrrrrrrrr
rrrrrrrrrrrrrrrrrrrrrrrrrrrrrrrrrrrrr
rrrrrrrrrrrrrrrrrrrrrrrrrrrrrrrrrrrrr
rrrrrrrrrrrrrrrrrrrrrrrrrrrrrrrrrrrrr
rrrrrrrrrrrrrrrrrrrrrrrrrrrrrrrrrrrrr
rrrrrrrrrrrrrrrrrrrrrrrrrrrrrrrrrrrrr
rrrrrrrrrrrrrrrrrrrrrrrrrrrrrrrrrrrrr
rrrrrrrrrrrrrrrrrrrrrrrrrrrrrrrrrrrrr
rrrrrrrrrrrrrrrrrrrrrrrrrrrrrrrrrrrrr
rrrrrrrrrrrrrrrrrrrrrrrrrrrrrrrrrrrrr
rrrrrrrrrrrrrrrrrrrrrrrrrrrrrrrrrrrrr
rrrrrrrrrrrrrrrrrrrrrrrrrrrrrrrrrrrrr
rrrrrrrrrrrrrrrrrrrrrrrrrrrrrrrrrrrrr
rrrrrrrrrrrrrrrrrrrrrrrrrrrrrrrrrrrrr
rrrrrrrrrrrrrrrrrrrrrrrrrrrrrrrrrrrrr
rrrrrrrrrrrrrrrrrrrrrrrrrrrrrrrrrrrrr
rrrrrrrrrrrrrrrrrrrrrrrrrrrrrrrrrrrrr
rrrrrrrrrrrrrrrrrrrrrrrrrrrrrrrrrrrrr
rrrrrrrrrrrrrrrrrrrrrrrrrrrrrrrrrrrrr
rrrrrrrrrrrrrrrrrrrrrrrrrrrrrrrrrrrrr
rrrrrrrrrrrrrrrrrrrrrrrrrrrrrrrrrrrrr
rrrrrrrrrrrrrrrrrrrrrrrrrrrrrrrrrrrrr
rrrrrrrrrrrrrrrrrrrrrrrrrrrrrrrrrrrrr
rrrrrrrrrrrrrrrrrrrrrrrrrrrrrrrrrrrrr
rrrrrrrrrrrrrrrrrrrrrrrrrrrrrrrrrrrrr
rrrrrrrrrrrrrrrrrrrrrrrrrrrrrrrrrrrrr
rrrrrrrrrrrrrrrrrrrrrrrrrrrrrrrrrrrrr
rrrrrrrrrrrrrrrrrrrrrrrrrrrrrrrrrrrrr
rrrrrrrrrrrrrrrrrrrrrrrrrrrrrrrrrrrrr
rrrrrrrrrrrrrrrrrrrrrrrrrrrrrrrrrrrrr
rrrrrrrrrrrrrrrrrrrrrrrrrrrrrrrrrrrrr
rrrrrrrrrrrrrrrrrrrrrrrrrrrrrrrrrrrrr
rrrrrrrrrrrrrrrrrrrrrrrrrrrrrrrrrrrrr

Life

life
may
be
defined
as
one
thing
stacked
upon
another
life
may
be
defined
as
one
thing
stacked
upon
another
life
may
be
defined
as
one
thing
stacked
upon
another
life

a

g

i

l

e

ANITAIN'TANITANITAIN'

N'TANITAANITAIN'TANIT

Wonder

When my dog watches me doing

something mechanical I sometimes

wonder if she sees the point of it all

Pairing

You can put a round peg in
a square hole and the same
for a square peg in a round
hole if the hole is big enough

Pearls

When pearls of wisdom became pearls of
stupidity it was like opening a bag of ancient
marbles counting them and tossing them away

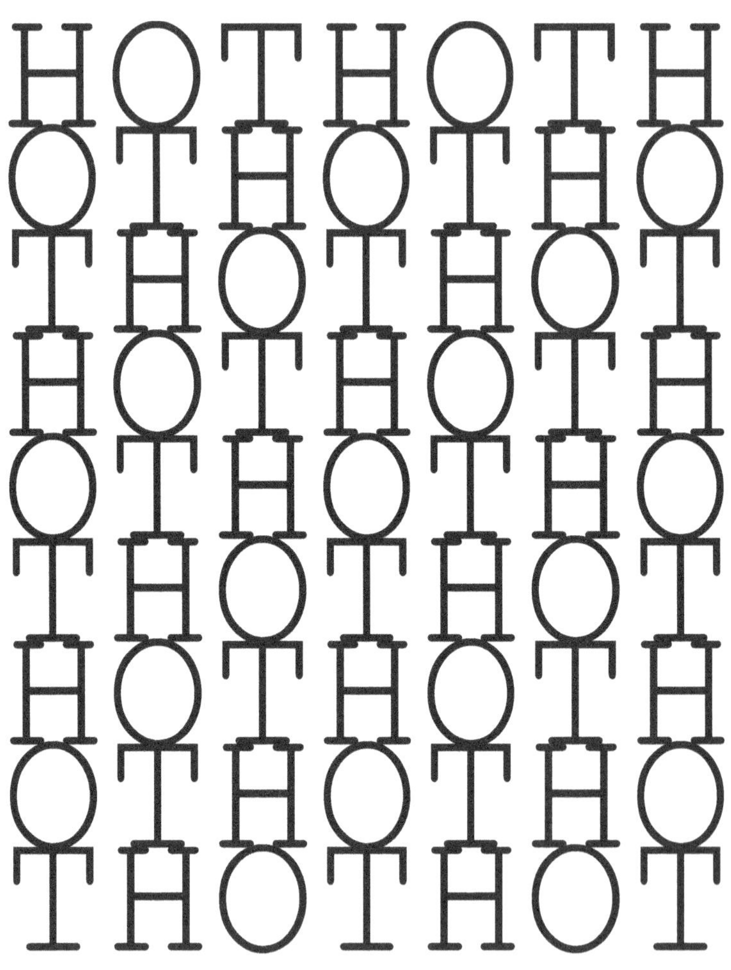

Spilling

Eventually in your life

you will spill red wine

if you haven't already
                    ‘
                    ‘
                    ‘
                    ‘
                    ‘
                    ‘
                    ‘
          ‘‘‘‘‘‘‘‘‘‘‘‘‘‘‘‘‘‘‘‘

Positive Preacher

A preacher said that in the afterlife
everyone encounters all the people
in their former lives but they only
have to be with the ones they love

Favorite Uncle

Everyone deserves a favorite uncle— the one that always gives you
a true answer to a question or insight into a problem you may have.
If you think this is trite you may never have had a favorite uncle.

Hark

Hark, it's the new year
new mornings are here
like undefiled senryu
arriving just for you
the year here to seize
turning rainforests to
burgers with cheese
what is there to say
new year on belay

When

Some things get fixed when they hurt, others
don't get fixed no matter how much they hurt
and then there is the inscrutable in-between

CCC
RRRRRRRRR
IIIIIIIIIIIIIIIIIIIIIIIIIIII
TTTTTTTTTTTTTTTTTTTT
IIIIIIIIIIIIIIIIIIIIIIIIIIIIIIII
CCCCCCCCCCCCCCCCCC
IIIIIIIIIIIIIIIIIIIIIIIIIIII
ZZZZZZZZZZZZZZ
EEEEEEEEE
DDD

Eternity

One time a guy sitting next to me in
church told me he was closest to eternity
when he was mugging in front of the mirror

Happy

There are certain ages
where people are more
likely to make you happy

Winner

Sometimes you have to be thankful for what you have

like the other day when I was talking to an old boy at

the park he told me his life had come down to him and

his dog and jug wine and said he was thankful for that

Heritage

Down the road of distant
ranches life is wholesome
among the tangled branches

Lady

An elderly lady sitting next to me in church told
me she had long ago said good-bye to her former
self but always kept her within hailing distance

CHEEK JOWLS

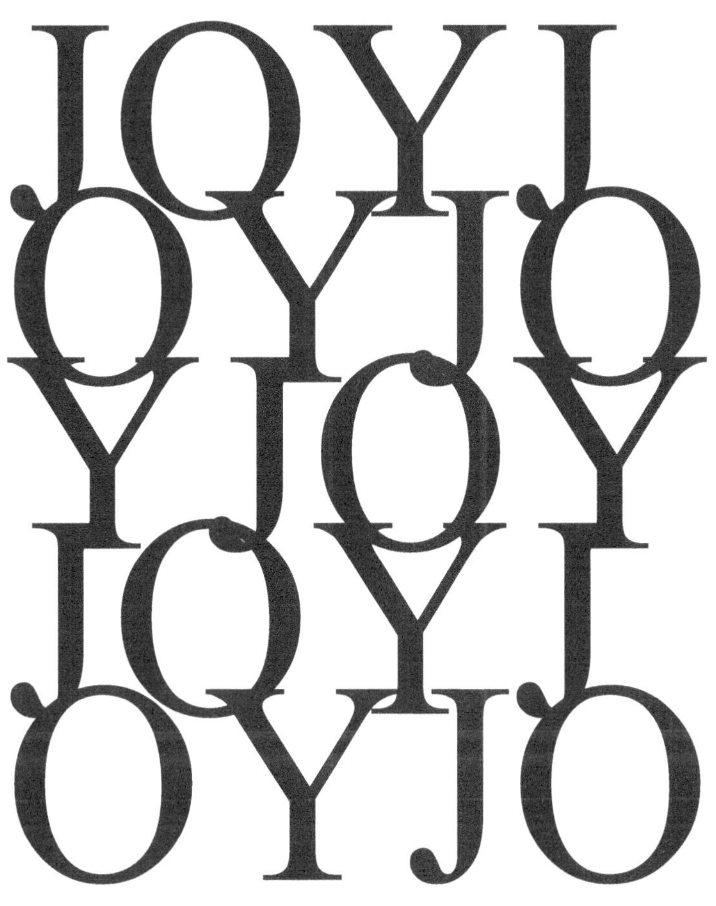

CREATURECOME
ORTSCREATURE
COMFORTSCREA
TURECOMFORTS
CREATURECOME
ORTSCREATURE
COMFORTSCREA
TURECOMFORTS
CREATURECOME
ORTSCREATURE
COMFORTSCREA
TURECOMFORTS

HA
RD

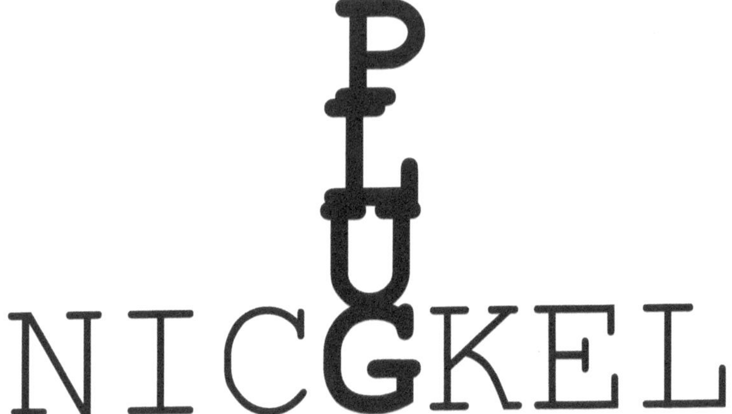
PLUG
NICGKEL

Support

A guy once told me that when he was
down and he ran out of friends to call
he would call his enemies for support

Nutrition

Proper nutrition
is for people who
are not starving
and for other
people as well

E   N   T   R   A   N   C   E

E   N   T   R   A   N   C   E

E   N   T   R   A   N   C   E

E   N   T   R   A   N   C   E

E   N   T   R   A   N   C   E

E   N   T   R   A   N   C   E

        T   R   A   N   C   E

E   N   T   R   A   N   C   E

‘ ‘ ‘ ‘ ‘ ‘ ‘ ‘ ‘ ‘

‘ ‘ ‘ ‘ ‘ ‘ ‘ ‘ ‘ ‘

‘ ‘ ‘ ‘ ‘ ‘ ‘ ‘ ‘ ‘

‘ ‘ ‘ ‘ ‘ ‘ ‘ ‘ ‘ ‘

‘ ‘ ‘ ‘ ‘ ‘ ‘ ‘ ‘ ‘

‘ ‘ ‘ ‘ ‘ ‘ ‘ ‘ ‘ ‘

‘ ‘ ‘ ‘ ‘ ‘ ‘ ‘ ‘ ‘

‘ ‘ ‘ ‘ ‘ ‘ ‘ ‘ ‘ ‘

‘ ‘ ‘ ‘ ‘ ‘ ‘ ‘ ‘ ‘

‘ ‘ ‘ ‘ ‘ Gus ‘ ‘ ‘ ‘ ‘

‘ ‘ ‘ ‘ ‘ ‘ ‘ ‘ ‘ ‘

‘ ‘ ‘ ‘ ‘ ‘ ‘ ‘ ‘ ‘

sTENTOR

End Of The Line

Your Initials

Snow Flurries

flurry flurry
flurry flurry flurry
flurry flurry

flurry flurry flurry
flurry flurry flurry flurry
flurry flurry flurry

flurry
flurry flurry
flurry

flurry flurry flurry
flurry flurry flurry flurry
flurry flurry flurry

flurry flurry
flurry flurry flurry
flurry flurry

Bum Steer

B U M

M I B

U I U

B I I 0 I I M

M I B

U I U

B I M

M U B

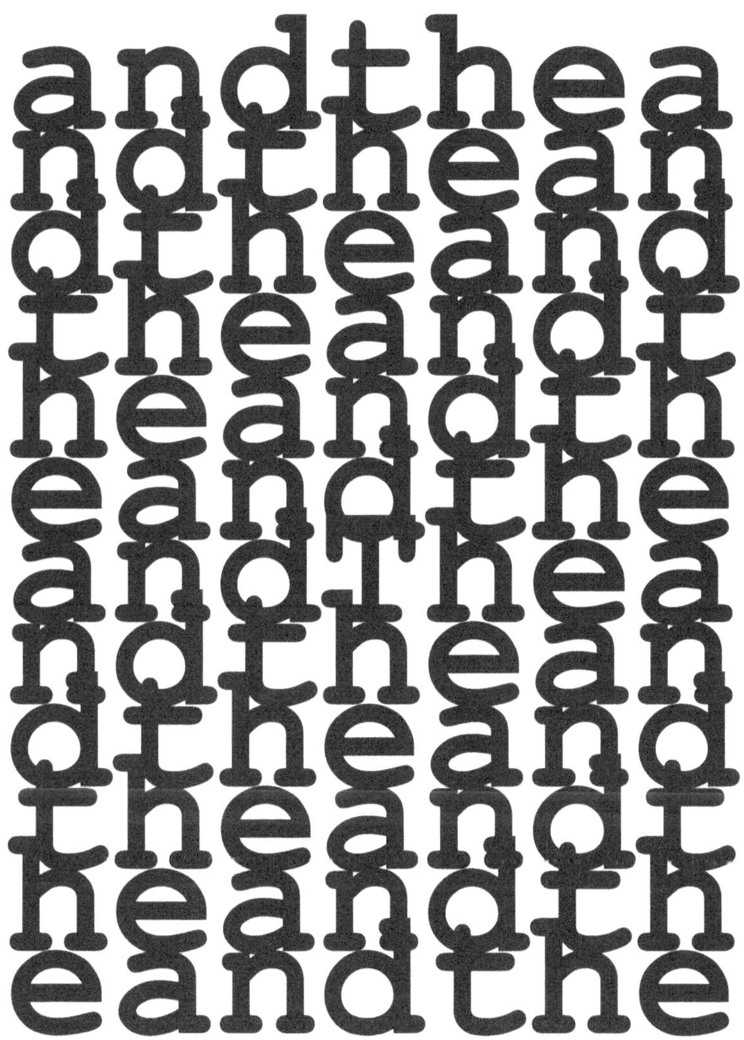

Gregarious

Orange

Shopper: I wonder what makes a good orange.

Grocer: Another good orange.

Shopper: I didn't mean it like that.

Grocer: Me either.

Quantum

Anyone who says you can't
live on chocolate chip cookies
has little grasp of quantum mechanics

Article

Happiness is rediscovering a long-forgotten
article of clothing that you needed badly and
were getting ready to shop for a replacement

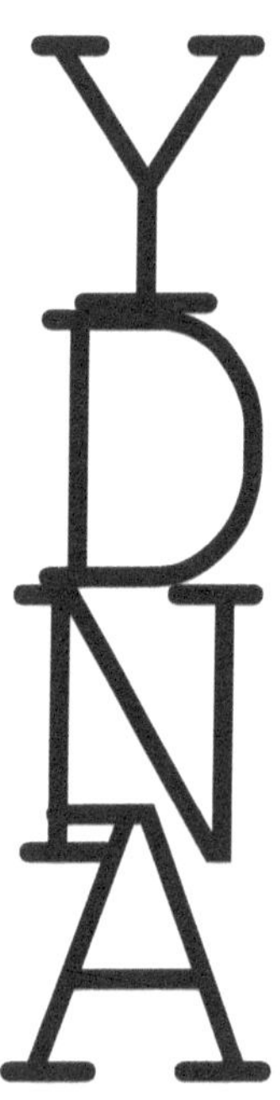
Y
D
R
N
A

Invoice

$ -00.0001

Double Jeopardizing

Q: What is a joke?

A: What is the question

GULFGULFGULF
GULFGULFGULF
GULFGULFGULF
GULFGULFGULF
GULFGENFGULF
GULFGULFGULF
GULFGULFGULF
GULFGULFGULF
GULFGULFGULF

Inseparable

At the end of the football
season some of us began
to look like our couches

Longevity

The secret to living to a
hundred years is to count
to a hundred very slowly

Tilt

Life is like a pin-ball game
and you need to always keep
reminding yourself not to tilt

Anew

Lost memories are gained anew
each moment of sight, sound, touch,
smell, taste, feeling, and thought

Populous

Looking at the new-fallen

snow wondering why some

flakes sparkle while others don't

Camp Pain

Slicing and dicing everything
in his path until the sharpener
confused him with his enemies

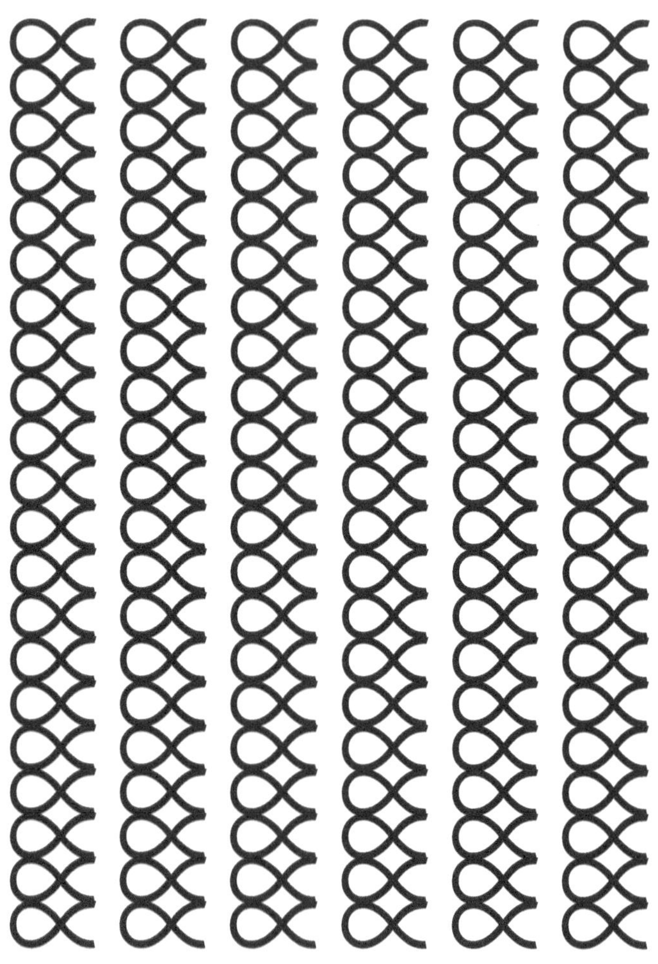

Crossing

One would think the shallow stuff

would be easier to get through but

it takes longer than anyone thinks

Living

Sometimes living a
part and living apart
are exactly the same

Shelter

There may be a reason
why serving food can be
the best thing there is to do

Mistake

~~Mistake~~

Correctness

Some corrections are
difficult to accept only
because they are correct

Jerk

In the schoolyard somebody called him a jerk. With time he grew to accept that pronouncement and the calming effect it had on him, ultimately leaving him with a feeling of ease and happiness.

Paperless Trail

If Cai Lun made the
first paper I wonder
who'll make the last

Pie Shop

With all the variety
society began to take
on a feeling of satiety
along with the piety

When

When nothing works
maybe the best thing
one can do is to play

Chuck

When the woodchuck starts

chucking the wood duck better

duck or he is plumb out of luck

Knobs

Years ago a friend had a steering wheel knob, sometimes called a suicide knob. He heard they were illegal and removed it, then found the heel of his hand served as a substitute in making turns easy, although not nearly as safe. It turns out knobs are legal.

Pierless

A gribble once gobbled up grauple
doing nothing for his inveterate waddle
nor for a peerless life most improbable

Deduction

In medieval times a   a times medieval In

self-stiled town fence   fence town self-stiled

allowed knowledgeable   knowledgeable allowed

residents to go scot-free   free-scot go to residents

Floaters

Friend I: You know those little specks I see
        in my eyes all the time?

Friend II: Yep , they're called floaters.

Friend I: Well, usually they're random and
        float all over the place but lately
        they are actually forming patterns,
        images and stuff.

Friend II: Never heard of that before but if
        they start giving you good tips on the
        stock market how about letting me know.

Friend I: You bet.

Vanishing

Some vanishing
creams take longer
than others to disappear

www.ingramcontent.com/pod-product-compliance
Lightning Source LLC
Chambersburg PA
CBHW020613160726
47991CB00002BA/752